Paranormal Australia

Alan Toner

Other Books by Alan Toner

True Ghost Stories
True Ghost Stories 2
True Ghost Stories 3
True Ghost Stories 4
100 True Ghost Stories
100 True Ghost Stories 2
Famous Psychics
Celebrity Hauntings
Haunted Objects
Hammer Horror Remembered
UK UFOs

Contents

1. The Princess Theatre

The Princess Theatre, situated on 163 Spring Street in Melbourne, Australia, is a 1488-seat venue. It was built in 1854 by the actor-manager George Coppin, who would go on to create Melbourne's theatre land. The Princess Theatre is the second building on the present site, the first being Astley's Amphitheatre, which opened in 1854.

Over the years, there have been several reported ghostly sightings in The Princess Theatre. On the evening of 3 March 1888, the baritone Frederick Baker, whose stage name was "Frederick Federici", was performing as Mephistopheles (another name for the Devil) in Gounod's opera Faust. This production ended with Mephistopheles plunging through a trapdoor and down to the fires of hell with his prize: the ill-fated Dr Faustus. As the captivated audience held its collective breath whilst watching Federici being lowered down through the stage into this basement, he tragically suffered a heart attack and died immediately, all the efforts of theatre staff to resuscitate him proving fruitless.

Totally shocked and saddened by this tragedy, they laid out his lifeless body on the floor, still clad in his crimson vestments. He never came back onstage to take the customary bows. When the company was summoned together to be informed that Federici had died, they asked, "When?" When they heard what had happened at the end of the opera, they said, "He's just been onstage and taken the bows with us." That was the just the first of the sightings. Since then, many people who have never heard of the Federici story have claimed to see a ghostly figure in evening dress at the theatre. For many years, the third-row seat in the dress circle was kept vacant as a tribute to him.

The ghost is usually seen in the dress circle and wandering the halls of the theatre. It is actually considered to be a good omen to see Federici's ghost on the opening night of a performance, so this is why people always leave a seat free in the dress circle for Federici to sit in. There actually was a recent play there that proved to be a financial flop and, as a result, ended up being cancelled. Some people think this is because Federici's spirit wasn't seen on the opening night. It has also been said that on the nights after Federici's death, the actor who took his role felt himself being pushed back whenever he tried to take the final bow.

When Kennedy Miller made a documentary nearly 80 years later, in the early 1970s, a photograph of the film set revealed an ashen-faced, semi-transparent observer. Nobody on the set saw the figure on that day; only the photograph revealed 'the ghost'.

It does seem highly appropriate that the Andrew Lloyd Webber musical, The Phantom of the Opera, should have had its Australian premiere at Melbourne's Princess Theatre in 1990, with a third Australian season in 2007, given the fact that The Princess Theatre has been compared to the Paris Opera, setting of the book and musical of Webber's production; and the Princess Theatre, where several opera productions have been staged, is reported to have its own resident spirit: a ghost that has been seen on several occasions.

2. Brisbane City Hall

Brisbane City Hall was opened by his Excellency the Governor Sir John Goodwin on the 8th April 1930. The site on which the City Hall now stands had been purchased in 1877. However, the site had been deemed unsuitable for a municipal hall in preference of a more elevated location.

Brisbane City Hall is said to be home to at least four ghosts: one ghost is a female and haunts the foyer area; one ghost is reported to haunt an entire wing of City Hall that was subsequently shut down for decades as a result, before being converted into a childcare centre; one ghost is alleged to be that of a WWII American sailor who engaged in a fight over a woman with another sailor, in which he was stabbed to death in the Red Cross Tea Rooms beneath City Hall. It is the fourth haunting, the Lift Attendant's phantom that haunts the tower of City Hall, that we shall discuss here.

Early in the building's history, around the 1930's, a lift attendant at City Hall perished in his dereliction of duty. There are, however, conflicting stories which claim he either fell, jumped, or was crushed by the lift during installation. Nobody really knows exactly how he came about his death, but it is widely acknowledged that his ghost does ride the elevator of the tower, and is even responsible for mechanical failures.

Over the years, many newspaper reporters and journalists have written various reports on the ghost. For example, in June 1998, the Queensland Independent reporter, Louise Rugendyke, reported that a ghost has been continually riding the lift since the 1930's. Ten years later, during renovations of City Hall, an article written by Kelmeny Fraser published in the City News stated that during renovation of the clock tower, a construction worker claimed to have seen a ghost in the form of a silhouette of a man standing in an area off-limits to the public. The following year, Nicole Carrington reported in the City News that among the ghosts of City Hall is that of a maintenance man who rides the lifts, and who is said to have died in a freak accident.

So is there any real truth behind all these reports of ghostly activity? Well, to find that out, we have to consider that the incident that most likely led to the story of the haunted tower occurred on no more a supernaturally appropriate day as Halloween. On the 31st of October 1935, building contractor George Edward Betts left his home in Bardon at about 7am on his way to work. At the time, he was working on a construction project erecting two workers' dwellings, and had seemed in good spirits when he'd left his wife for the day. On his departure, he had mentioned to her that he planned to visit the doctor on the way to work, and at some stage during the day would need to visit City Hall to pay Council for water connection work at a building site in Annerley. George worked throughout the morning on-site, before changing his clothes at lunchtime and informing the other builders that he needed to go into town on business.

Around 2:15pm at the City Hall, Liftman George Jones accepted two passengers for a trip to the observation landing of the tower: a man (George Betts) and a woman, neither of whom appeared to know the other. About five minutes later, the woman entered the lift once more and was taken back down to the ground floor. A couple of minutes passed, during which George Betts was left all alone on the observation landing. It's anybody guess as to what actually happened at the top of the tower during those short few

4

minutes. However, a loud crash was heard by those on the lower levels of the Hall soon after. On investigation, a large hole could be seen in the roof of the Hall facing King George Square. A subsequent room search resulted in the discovery of George's body - he had plummeted over 40 metres from the observation landing, through the galvanised iron roof of City Hall, coming to rest on the concrete floor of a chamber off the record room. His brief bag was later located alongside the telescope at the top of the tower.

An inquest was conducted shortly after the accident, at which a number of witnesses were summoned. The safety of the observation landing was immediately questioned: were the installed safety railings sufficient to prevent sightseers from accidentally falling from the tower? Evidence was provided that it would not be possible for a sightseer to fall over the rail whilst on the observation landing. Constable Fursman of the Brisbane Police provided testimony that he had thoroughly examined the safety rail, and claimed that it would be "impossible" for anyone to fall over the grill support near the telescope under ordinary conditions, unless he climbed upon it. In the policeman's opinion, there were no suspicious circumstances surrounding the death. Consequently, the inquest was closed.

There are still many unanswered questions as to what exactly possessed George Betts to climb over the safety rail leading to his fatal fall. Perhaps he had been given bad news about his health during his visit to the doctor earlier that morning, thus possibly driving him towards taking his own life later that afternoon. Who knows?

3. Victoria Park Railway Tunnel

Victoria Park Railway Tunnel in Brisbane, Australia, was the subject of one of Brisbane's most famous phantoms in 1965, after a group of local children overheard rumours that a ghost had been observed within the tunnel.

During the following evening, the brave young ghost hunters crept down in the hope of glimpsing this entity. One boy, who trailed behind the rest of the group as they passed through the tunnel, was apparently approached by a misty green, limbless and headless apparition that seemed to materialise from the wall of the tunnel. Seemingly hypnotised by the spook, the boy was solicitously dragged by his friends to the nearby Royal Brisbane Hospital, as his companions feared he had been possessed by the ghost.

The children's account to hospital staff of the ghost hit the newspaper headlines the next day, and very soon thousands of local residents converged on both sides of the tunnel in the hope of catching a glimpse of the spook. Throughout the next week, the Victoria Park ghost became the major talking point of Brisbane, and various theories as to its true identity were put forward. However, the ghost may well have been that of one of the numerous suicides that had taken place in Victoria Park in previous years.

4. Dreamworld Theme Park

Dreamworld is a large theme park situated on the Gold Coast, Coomera, Queensland. It is currently Australia's largest theme park, with over 40 rides and attractions, including five roller coasters.

A certain building inside the grounds of the theme park, where the reality television series Big Brother Australia is produced, has been reported to be haunted since the show's start in 2001. Many production staff have witnessed the apparition of a young girl, as well as a child's voice and fog appearing late at night and early in the morning.

5. Monte Cristo Homestead

Monte Cristo Homestead in Junee, New South Wales, was the site of seven deaths in the 1800s, and is reported to be the most haunted house in Australia. This historic two-story house, with its wide verandas and ornate wrought iron work, stands on a hill overlooking the town, and is now open to thousands of visitors each year - and they all want to know about the ghosts and tragedies connected with this sprawling mansion. Various paranormal groups have reported many strange phenomena there: ghostly figures, strange lights, invisible force fields, phantom sounds and even animal mutilations. These are attributed to several tragic incidents in the property's past, including the murder of a caretaker in 1961 and the imprisonment of a mentally impaired man for many years in the dairy. During the Crawleys' occupation, a young child is said to have been dropped down the stairs to his death, a maid to have fallen from the balcony, and a stable boy to have been burnt to death.

Over the years, the Monte Cristo Homestead has been investigated by many ghost hunters. It has also been featured on the world famous Castle of Spirits website as one of their favourite haunts. The Australian Ghost Hunters Society regularly holds ghost hunts at Monte Cristo, and has had some very interesting experiences there.

The original occupants were William Crawley and his family in 1884, and indeed it is from the Crawley family themselves that most of the stories of ghosts and hauntings, and many other tragic happenings, seem to originate. In fact, the ghost of old Mrs Crawley, the most dominant spirit there, has been seen many times in her former room. It is believed that after William Crawley died in 1910, from a carbuncle on his neck becoming infected by his starched collar, Mrs Crawley only left the house on two occasions in the remaining 23 years of her life. It is, therefore, small wonder that her presence still lingers. There have also been many reports of mysterious lights and apparitions.

Not surprisingly, given all these ghostly reports, the Monte Cristo has become quite a popular tourist attraction with visitors to Australia over the years.

The most recent death at Monte Cristo occurred in 1961, when caretaker Jackie Simpson was murdered by a local youth. After watching the movie Psycho several times, the boy made his way up to the grounds of the homestead with a rifle and shot the caretaker dead in his cottage. It is believed that he then scrawled the words "DIE JACK HA HA" on the wooden door, a macabre inscription that can still be seen to this day.

Monte Cristo's reputation for being haunted is well known within Australia, thanks partially to several television shows, including segments on the property. These include the current-affairs show Big Country in 1977, the travel show Getaway in 1992, the paranormal based game/reality show Scream Test in 2000, and Ghost Hunters International 14 January 2010.

There are many more spooky stories and ghostly sightings at Monte Cristo, and for anybody with a keen interest in haunted buildings, the place is definitely worth a visit. The homestead is open daily for tours, and a book about the paranormal occurrences is available from the gift shop.

6. Whepstead House

Whepstead House, situated in Wellington Point, Queensland, is an historic weatherboard mansion designed to catch cool breezes coming off Moreton Bay, and set in expansive lawns and gardens. Today it is a popular restaurant and function centre.

Whepstead House is reported to have a number of ghosts: Gilbert Burnett's wife Martha, who emanates the scent of lavender perfume; the daughter of Gilbert and Martha, who apparently disappeared without trace; Gilbert and Martha's son, who had a withered leg and haunts the stairwell; and the ghost of an elderly servant, who is seen around the house wearing a bowler's hat and suit.

All these apparitions have been witnessed by owners, staff and guests at 'Whepstead' in the past twenty years, and strange but harmless things happen regularly in the old house: candles are lit by unseen hands, stains appear and disappear on a large carpet, cheques left lying about have been concealed in a book, and on one occasion a heavy glass decanter stopper was hurled right across a room.

Whilst not one of these stories has any real historic basis, the house itself was used as a private hospital for a couple of decades, during which time more than a dozen people passed away. Therefore, it's perfectly possible that its paranormal atmosphere and strange occurrences stem from this period in its history.

7. Beechworth Lunatic Asylum

Originally known as Mayday Hills Lunatic Asylum, Beechworth Lunatic Asylum, is a decommissioned psychiatric hospital situated in Beechworth, a town of Victoria, Australia. Mayday Hills Lunatic Asylum was the fourth such Hospital to be built in Victoria and is one of the three largest. Mayday Hills Hospital closed in 1995 after 128 years of operation, and since then has operated as a campus of La Trobe University, run as a hotel and conference centre.

The most frequently seen ghost at the asylum is that of Matron Sharpe. Her apparition has been seen in several different parts of the hospital, especially in the former dormitory area, which is now part of Latrobe University's computer rooms. People have seen her phantom walking down the granite staircase and into one of the classrooms. Matron Sharpe was apparently very compassionate toward the patients, a personality trait which was, sadly, not very common in that particular period in history.

Another ghost said to haunt Beechworth is that of former patient Tommy Kennedy. Tommy was popular at the hospital and was given a job as a kitchen hand. He actually died in the kitchen, which is now part of the Bijou theatre. It is here that people have said they have felt someone tugging at their clothes or poking them in the ribs.

Two more ghosts are reported to haunt The Reaction Hall: one is of a young girl, who approaches women and tries to communicate with them; the other is an elderly man, who has been seen in a window that was once part of the Bell Tower.

There are two common sightings in the Grevillia Wing, which was the section of the hospital that most patients feared, as that was where various - and often extremely unpleasant - tests were performed on them (e.g. electro shock treatment, straitjacket restraint etc.). One ghost is thought to be that of an unknown male doctor, whose apparition has been seen wandering the corridors late at night. The other entity is Matron Sharpe, whose spirit was often seen in this area by the nurses who worked at Mayday Hills. They would report seeing the Matron sitting with patients who were due to have electro-shock treatment. Witnesses of this say that although the room grew icy cold, her presence was comforting to the patients, and seemed to alleviate their anxieties.

Workmen at the hospital have reported hearing the sound of children laughing and playing. When they investigate the sound, they are unable to find anybody there. Several years ago, on a ghost tour, a parent noticed their 10-year-old son talking to himself. When they asked who he was talking to, the boy said he was talking to a boy called James, who lived there.

Another ghostly tale involves a patient, a woman who was a heavy smoker. She was unceremoniously thrown out of a window to her death by another patient, who wanted her cigarettes. As the woman was Jewish, her body was not allowed to be moved until a Rabbi had seen it, so it was just left lying out the front of the hospital for two whole days until the Rabbi arrived from Melbourne. Her ghost has been seen on the spot where she fell by a number of people.

In the gardens of Beechworth, the ghost of a man wearing a green woollen jacket has been seen. The spook is thought to be that of a gardener named Arthur, who worked in the gardens for many years, earning ten shillings a week for his labour. He wore his green jacket in winter and summer, and would remove it for nobody. After Arthur died, it was discovered why Arthur had been discreetly storing his wages in the seam of his jacket. When the nurses opened it, they found 140 pounds - over four years of his wages - hidden inside.

Finally, the ghost of another patient - a man who mysteriously disappeared and could not be found anywhere by staff, despite exhaustive searching - has been seen near the entrance of the Asylum. These sightings often occur in the early hours of the morning. The story goes that the missing man's body was finally located up a tree, minus one leg, which had been caused to drop off by advanced decomposition. It was only by virtue of the resident dog being found chewing a leg near the gate house at the ground's entrance that the staff managed to trace the man's rotting corpse at all.

8. Studley Park House

Studley Park House, located in Narellan, NSW, and built in 1889, is reputed to be one of Australia's most haunted houses. It has been the subject of many medium investigations and is well familiar to many paranormal investigators.

Studley Park House is reported to be haunted by 14-year-old Ray Blackstone, who drowned in a nearby damn on 15th October 1909. His lifeless body was said to have been carried back to the house and kept in the cellar to await certification and burial.

In 1939, the son of then owner Arthur Adolphus Gregory died of appendicitis in the theatrette. Again a boy's body lay in wait in this house.

The presence of ghostly children has often been felt throughout the house, and in the tower stands the spirit of a lonely woman, awaiting the return of her man.

9. Gawler House

Gawler house in Gawler, South Australia, is reportedly haunted by previous tenants. One visitor has reported feeling a choking sensation upon entering the house.

10. Ghosts of Picton

The small rural town of Picton lies approximately 80 kilometres southwest of Sydney. The town's history can be traced as far back as 1798, when the land was first explored by Europeans wanting to settle further inland. The town was officially founded in 1822, when Major Henry Colden Antill was given the first land grant. Formerly known as Stonequarry, the town's name was changed to Picton in 1841, supposedly after Sir Thomas Picton, one of the Duke of Wellington's generals at the Battle of Waterloo.

Over the years, there have been many strange stories about St Mark's Church and Pioneer Graveyard. For instance, a woman parked in her car nearby spotted a young boy and girl holding hands and walking around the graves. After about ten minutes, the children mysteriously disappeared behind the headstones. Shortly afterwards, it occurred to the woman that the children had been dressed in old-fashioned clothes. There have been several other reports of these ghostly children. There have also been stories of a small girl, clad in white, wandering aimlessly through the cemetery late at night.

There have also been reports of a large dog prowling around the area, an entity which has harassed and frightened quite a few visitors over the years. Some believe this spectral hound to be the ghost of a minister's faithful St Bernard, which is buried in the church grounds.

Ghosts are also said to walk the historic Imperial Hotel, which was built in the 1860's and was originally called The Terminus, Picton being the terminus for the railway from 1863 until 1867. Various members of staff have reported the feeling of someone following them through a few rooms in the building. There is also

16

the equally strange story of a jukebox suddenly starting up and playing of its own accord.

The phantom of a woman is often seen in the window of the old semi detached Emmett Cottages. Shop owners often discover their displays have been mysteriously moved overnight.

There have also been reports of crying babies and the ghost of an unpleasant matron in Picton's beautiful old maternity hospital. People staying at the residence complain of being woken up in the middle of the night by invisible hands wrapped around their throats.

The sounds of people swimming and splashing in the water have been heard by locals at the beautiful Stonequarry Viaduct, which is the oldest stone railway viaduct still in use today. Over the years, many people drowned in the creek. Could those strange sounds be those of the unfortunate victims of the creek?

Wendover House, the Georgian mansion built in 1880 by John Wright McQuiggin, the first mayor of Picton, has a long history of paranormal phenomena. One former resident claims to have been visited several times by the ghost of McQuiggan, who he recognised from an old photograph. The building is now a block of flats.

The Redbank Range Railway Tunnel, more commonly known as the Picton Tunnel, has a very creepy aspect about it, and has quite a reputation for strange phenomena. For example, weird glowing lights have often been seen floating through and around the tunnel. It is also said to be haunted by the ghost of a woman who was killed by a train in 1916.

Wollondilly Shire Hall, formerly known as the Lower Picton School, is reported to be haunted by three ghosts: a bearded man wearing a hat and suit, a small mischievous boy, and a little girl, who is heard more than she is seen.

Razorback Inn, whose construction was completed by ex-convict Oliver Whiting in 1850, is the subject of many strange stories, and is home to an extremely noisy ghost.

11. National Film and Sound Archive

The National Film and Sound Archive, a grand art decor building located in Canberra, is a treasure trove of fascinating images and sounds considered worthy of preservation for future posterity. The collection ranges from works created in the late nineteenth century, when the recorded sound and film industries were in their infancy, to those made in the present day. Until 1984, it operated as the Australian Institute of Anatomy, where body parts were kept and collected.

Some people believe the ghosts of the dead still haunt the hallways of the building. The downstairs corridor in particular, which once housed hundreds of human skulls, is said to be rife with poltergeist activity. In the early 1990s, security and administration staff were called out to the building at about 2am as the sensors in this "corridor of death" had detected movement. No logical explanation for the movement was ever given. Also, a contractor claims to have been pinned against a wall in the basement by an unexplained presence. And if you visit the library, the ghost of a woman who stands silently in the balconies may watch you. She has been seen by staff and visitors alike.

Other paranormal phenomena reported here include a poltergeist that hurls the circular metal containers of the old-fashioned film strips, a Petri dish-throwing poltergeist in an upstairs darkroom, and the ghostly apparition of a child looking up through a grill in the old cinema.

It is not known exactly when the hauntings commenced, or

whether it was during the time of the Anatomy Institutes occupation of the building. Could the spirits be those of some of the bodies that were examined in the buildings basement/morgue?

12. The Fremantle Arts Centre

The Fremantle Arts Centre, whose construction is based on Gothic design, is one of the best-known haunted buildings in Western Australia. It used to be a mental asylum before it became a women's refuge centre. It was built solely by convicts. Both visitors and staff there have made countless reports over the years of a ghostly presence, cold spots, apparitions and even physical contact (e.g. being kissed on the cheek or the feeling of being pushed along the staircase). Most of the paranormal activity, according to staff, occurs on the first floor and in and around a couple of particular rooms on the same level.

It is said that when the building was an asylum, a woman who had been admitted here after her daughter's kidnapping slipped into a state of chronic depression and committed suicide by jumping from a first floor window. According to local legend, she is still looking for her child in the building.

Outside the front of the museum, the Court Yard has also had numerous reported sightings of ghostly apparitions dressed in old traditional clothing, walking around and seen sitting on the benches. During its asylum days in the mid to late 19th century, the current Court Yard was used as an exercise yard.

Paranormal groups who have investigated the building strongly believe it to be a hotbed of paranormal activity, and one of a few places in the world where you are almost certain to encounter some form of ghostly occurrence.

13. Port Arthur

In 1833 Port Arthur, situated in Tasmania, became a prison settlement for male convicts, which were predominantly British and Irish second offenders. Hundreds of inmates died in those early years, and many people believe that some of the spirits of those long-departed souls still linger around the place to this day.

The prison was even compared to Alcatraz due to its escape-proof structure, and just like those inmates of Alcatraz, many of the convicts at Port Arthur proved just how defiant and arrogant they were, as they found various ways of escaping back to outside world.

Inside the Commandant's House, the first house built in Port Arthur, sits a rocking chair known as the "Nanny Chair". This chair is said to be haunted. Witnesses have seen it rock of its own accord, and those who have sat on it have been touched by unseen hands or have strange feelings come over them. Frequently, those who try to photograph this chair experience equipment failure.

The Parsonage is believed to be one of the most haunted buildings in Port Arthur. A Reverend George Eastman died in an upstairs bedroom. While trying to lower his body, within a coffin, out of a window, the rope broke, the coffin flew open and his body fell in to a gutter. Witnesses have reported smelling a foul stench. They have also heard moaning noises and seen strange lights in the building ever since. A woman in a blue period dress has also been seen wandering the building. Ghostly entities have also been witnessed in the Junior Medical Officer's residence. It is believed his children are the perpetrators of footsteps, moving furniture and rattling windows. Private Robert Young drowned near the Jetty Cabin in 1840. Guests reported seeing a man with straight black hair and a ruffled white shirt in or near the cabin.

Strange faces popping out of a hole in the wall, only to disappear moments later, have been witnessed in the dissection rooms under the Senior Surgeon's House. This was the hole where the servants used to scrape the ashes from the fireplace down into the dissection room to soak up the blood. In the Separate Prison, visitors have heard the chilling screams of a phantom boy awaiting execution. In the same cell that William Carter hung himself, people have felt anxious or depressed. Mysterious lights have also been spotted in the dark cells where prisoners were incarcerated for long periods of time, in total darkness and silence.

Port Arthur's cemetery also has its own paranormal reports. A prisoner named Mark Jeffrey, serving time for manslaughter, lived on the island in a little hut as the resident gravedigger. One morning, the authorities spotted a signal fire, and a boat was immediately dispatched to retrieve Jeffrey. When he returned to the mainland, he told a very strange story. The night before, his hut had been shaken by some invisible force, and a fiery red glow had lit up the walls and surrounding ground. Upon investigation, he was confronted by an entity with smouldering eyes, large horns and encircled by sulphurous smoke. People gave little credence to his story, but some visitors have reported feeling an oppressive atmosphere on the Island of the Dead, which is small wonder, considering all the people who are buried there.

14. Redbank Range Tunnel

The Red Bank Range Tunnel - also known as the Picton or Mushroom Tunnel - was opened in February 1867 and is the first one to be used by the NSW Railways. It was eventually closed in 1919 when the new deviation line opened. During World War II, it was one of a number of disused railway tunnels used to store ammunition and other military supplies. The tunnel has also been used for professional mushroom growing after 1950, when the RAAF moved out.

The Red Bank Range Tunnel is 592 ft long, and has been the centre of much paranormal activity over the years. For example, strange glowing lights have been seen floating through and around the tunnel. Also, strange disembodied voices, icy temperatures and sudden inexplicable breezes, like those generated by an approaching train, have been experienced.

The spirit of a woman named Emily Bollard, who was struck and killed by a train in 1916, is reported to haunt the tunnel.

Should you feel inclined to wander down to The Redbank Range Railway Tunnel for perhaps a spot of ghost hunting, please be aware that the tunnel is located on private property. Police patrol the area regularly and anyone found trespassing will be asked to leave, and may even be charged. You can only access the tunnel legally through Liz Vincent's Picton Ghost Hunts or Tunnel Watches.

15. Waterfall Gully Restaurant

Waterfall Gully Restaurant is located in the foothills of the Mount Lofty Ranges around 5 km (3.1 mi) south-east of the Adelaide city centre. It was constructed between 1911 and 1912 by South Australian architects Albert Selmar Conrad and his brother Frank, and was formally opened by Sir Day Bosanquet on 9th November 1912. Its initial function was as a kiosk and tea rooms. It was later renovated into a restaurant in the 1950's and remains pretty much the same today. Built in the style of a Swiss chalet, the building has been heritage-listed since 1987. It is currently known as 'Utopia'.

There have been many reports about a ghostly fire fighter, clad in a blue uniform, being seen in and around the restaurant, and here is the story from which these reports have stemmed.

Around midday on Wednesday 16th December 1926, a fire broke out in the surrounding bush and threatened to spread to a number of local businesses and residences. It actually came to within yards of the Waterfall Gully kiosk, but was quelled around 5pm.

Unfortunately, a young constable with the Burnside Police, Thomas Tregoweth, fell down a hill, rolling through the flames and sustaining horrific burns and injuries. He sadly died from his injuries several days later. He was survived by a young wife and two-year-old son.

Just a few years later, in the early 1930's, Tregoweth's spirit was reportedly seen about the restaurant and the hillside where he died. It has also been seen wandering around the surrounding bush land. He still wears his uniform and seems to still be watching over the restaurant. His ghost does appear to be relatively harmless.

However, those walking the nearby trails at night don't really think so, and get a rather different impression. They often experience a strong feeling of foreboding and unease, and those who actually see the ghostly figure say his body seems to radiate a bright, fiery light.

Even the Waterfall Gully owner, Justin Markos, says he and other staff have experienced strange, unexplained happenings, from mysteriously moving items to late-night whistling when there's nobody else around.

The spirit of Constable Tregoweht is also known as "The Blue Ghost", due to the fact that he is always seen wearing his distinctive blue police uniform.

16. Old Geelong Gaol

The historic Geelong Gaol, which is a Heritage listed site, is a top attraction for anyone remotely interested in Australia's early penal history during the nation's establishment as a British colony. It is also a highly recommended place to visit for anybody with a keen interest in ghosts and spirits.

A four-storey edifice, the gaol was first occupied in 1853. The British Pentonville Prison inspired its design, and it was built by convicts who were incarcerated in ship hulks moored in Corio Bay. A total of six convicts were hanged in Geelong from 1854 to 1865. Four of these occurred at Gallows Flat on October 28 1865. The gaol was operated as a high security prison until it was decommissioned in July 1991.

Prisoners were held in extremely uncomfortable and unhygienic conditions, in tiny, unheated cells, with no proper sewerage facilities, for up to fourteen hours each day. Such appalling conditions made the place seem more like some grim, dark dungeon than a prison.

Geelong Gaol remains more or less the same today as it was when it closed down. Some exhibits of its history have been added, giving it the aspect of a museum. However, the gaol itself continues to present a formidable and anxiety-inducing sight to anybody who travels near it.

As to what manner of paranormal activity has been experienced in the prison, previous inmates have reported hearing strange female cries late at night, especially in the East Wing, where the Industrial School for Girls was situated in the late 1860s. Also, tour guides have witnessed several paranormal occurrences, including swirling mists, general unpleasant feelings and people being physically assaulted by unseen entities.

Various paranormal research teams investigating the site have experienced strange mists, weird sounds, EMF anomalies and orbs. Some mediums and similarly psychic people have reported the presence of various spirits in the gaol. The old infirmary, cell 45, the gallows, and the external shower block are the areas where the paranormal activity has been especially rife.

The Rotary Club of Geelong has now taken charge of the Geelong, and frequently runs guided tours during weekends and holidays.

17. St. John's Orphanage

St. John's Orphanage, situated in Goulburn, New South Wales, was opened in 1905 by the Sisters of Mercy and The Catholic Church, with the foundation stone laid and blessed on the 17th of March by Bishop Gallagher of Goulburn. It was one of the first orphanages to be built in Goulburn. For the period 1905 until 1912, St. John's was home to both males and females. In 1912 St. Joseph's House of Prayer was opened, and this became Goulburn's girls' orphanage.

The building closed in 1976, after 71 years in service. It is said to be haunted by a number of spirits.

The orphanage is now, sadly, run down and bears extensive damage caused by years of heavy vandalism.

Nocturnal ghost tours are regularly conducted by a local company.

18. Devil's Pool

Devil's pool, also known as Babinder Boulders, is a small body of water located under a small waterfall in Geelong, Victoria. The area is said to be cursed due to all the deaths that have occurred there over the years.

Local legend has it that a son of an early settler to the area in the 1800's fell off the cliff and into Devil's Pool, where he drowned. It is said that if you go there at night, you can hear a small child sobbing.

Another legend arises from the story of a woman who married a respected tribal elder, but ran away with a beautiful young man visiting for the event. When they were captured, she threw herself into the waters to escape, calling for her lover to follow her. The legend has it that her spirit guards the boulders, and that her calls for her lover can still be heard.

Local Aboriginal people believe that when people disrespect the site, the site reciprocates that disrespect. One story concerns a man who was warned, but kicked the plaque, slipped into the hole and drowned where a body had just been recovered. There is another story of a drowned man whose father photographed the site in memoriam. When the photograph was developed, the son's face appeared on the rocks. He's even got the cigarette still stuck in his mouth.

The Aboriginal people, among them Rainforest people, feel they are protected and anyone who goes there with them as friends are also protected.

On 30th November 2008, Tasmanian naval seaman James Bennett became the seventeenth person to drown at the site since 1959.

In November 2009, a woman claimed a photo she took at the site showed what appeared to be a ghost in the water.

19. The Pub Poltergeist

At a certain pub in Geelong West, called Irish Murphy's, frequent poltergeist activity has been reported by both staff and contractors.

The ghost is known as "Mary", and is apparently behind all the paranormal activity that has occurred at the pub. Glasses have been hurled across rooms, urns have been moved, doors have been slammed, menu dockets have been ejected from printers, phones have been set ringing, and spine-chilling voices have hissed into the ears of customers and staff.

The pub used to be known as the Argyle Hotel and was built in 1865. It also incurred the name "The Strangler's Arms" due to the fact that a woman was strangled upstairs in the 1950s. Nobody knows for sure whether it was actually Mary or an earlier inhabitant.

One night, the publican's daughter was working alone in the pub, and rang her mother in hysterics, complaining that she had just witnessed the ghost of Mary. The girl claimed that the small salt and pepper containers started jiggling on their own, and somebody whispered into her ear. The girl was so shaken up by her weird experience that she could not recall exactly what that disembodied voice said.

The publican herself also had an encounter with the Mary entity. During the day renovations on the building commenced, she witnessed four glasses flying sideways from a table and into a nearby wall. She then saw another, equally strange thing: dockets started spewing out of the kitchen computer, hitting the wall and everywhere else.

Even the building supervisor had a strange experience. One night, when he returned, he noticed that all the lights were switched on – even though they'd all been turned off – and he heard strange, loud noises coming from the toilet. He was too scared to investigate the source of the commotion.

The publican called in ghost hunter Jo Howell, who suggested that Mary was possibly displeased by changes to the pub, and with herself for staying. The paranormal activity then stopped.

However, Mary's ghost hadn't gone forever, for some time later a customer was drinking at the bar when he suddenly felt a tap on his shoulder. Looking around and seeing nobody there, he then turned to the publican and said: "She's back."

Since then, Mary's ghost has resumed its spooking of customers and staff.

20. The Guyra Ghost

One of the most famous ghost stories in Australia's history – and perhaps the most controversial - is that of the Guyra Ghost. In fact, the case became such a media sensation that it also inspired a movie.

The case of the Guyra Ghost – or, to be more precise, Poltergeist – began in the home of William Bowen and his family in April 1921. Loud thumping sounds were heard on the walls, followed by showers of stones, which eventually shattered every window in the tiny weatherboard cottage just outside Guyra. Although nobody could identify who or what was responsible for these disturbances, it soon became evident that the attacks seemed to be focused on 12-year-old Minnie. Stones smashed through her bedroom window, thrown by unseen hands, and fell on her bed.

As it turned out, one of the Bowen children admitted to tossing some rocks on the roof to frighten a younger sibling, but this didn't seem to account for all of the paranormal activity, especially as these things kept occurring even when policemen where nearby. Local residents – many of who had observed the phenomena at the Bowen's – became quite nervous. Some even took to sleeping with loaded guns at hand. One young girl was wounded in the head and several other people narrowly escaped being shot. The local police sergeant, who sat up every night at the cottage amid the constant thumps and showers of stones, finally broke under the strain, and was sent away for a 'rest'.

The Guyra Ghost case even generated much international interest. One of the people attracted to the remote township by the mystery was a Mr Moors, a personal friend of Sir Arthur Conan

Doyle, who shared his interest in the paranormal. When he was granted full access to the house, Moors removed parts of the roof to create vantage points and set up an elaborate network of traps. However, as if in defiance of this, the ghost continued its troublesome activity. Moors and his five assistants were completely bemused, as they couldn't even say for sure whether the walnut-sized stones were thrown from inside or outside the house. But where the foreign expert failed, a local ghost-buster may have partially succeeded.

When Ben Davey of Uralla, a student of spiritualism, visited the Bowen household, he discovered that May, a daughter of Mrs Bowen's by a former marriage, had died about three months earlier. He immediately suspected the spirit of the dead girl was trying to communicate with young Minnie. After a spate of knockings, a tearful Minnie confessed that May had indeed spoken to her, telling her "not to worry," as she would watch over and guard them all. Subsequently, all poltergeist activity ceased, at least for the moment. But when the thumping noises and stone-falls flared up again, Minnie's parents, in desperation, sent her to her grandmother's house in Glen Innes, 60 kilometres away. The fact that she really had been the focus of the entity's attention was soon confirmed, as it followed her there and continued its unearthly antics.

The second house was situated in town, but the wall-shuddering thumps were still hard to explain. The force of some of the thumps was that powerful that they even dislodged ornaments on a sideboard. When a 200-pound man threw his full weight against the wall next to the sideboard, the ornaments did not even shake.

Eventually, Minnie's parents brought her back to the

35

Guyra cottage. After that, apparently, the strange phenomena simply abated.

Twelve-year-old Minnie appears to have been a typical poltergeist target: the kind of troubled adolescent who frequently is the focus, and possibly the unconscious instigator, of a mischievous spirit.

The two houses where the paranormal activity happened still stand, although the Bowen residence has been enlarged and renovated. The current occupants, though a little nervous when they first moved in after hearing all the stories about the house being haunted, have experienced no ghostly occurrences whatsoever.

When Minnie Bowen grew up, she married and became Mrs Inks. She lived for many more years, with no further paranormal occurrences in her life, in Armidale.

In later life, she is not recorded as mentioning anything more about The Guyra Ghost than what had already been documented. Around 1988 or '89, the elderly lady was run over and killed, just outside Armidale.

In 1921, a silent movie was made about the incident, entitled 'The Guyra Ghost Mystery'. John Cosgrove starred in and directed the film. The Bowens themselves appeared in the picture.

21. King George Avenue

Over the years, King George Avenue in Tamworth has gained a reputation for being an area where paranormal activity has occurred.

For instance, there have been numerous reports about ghostly headlights appearing to people who are driving in the direction of the city. Also, random electrical problems - like fuses suddenly blowing - have occurred quite often.

The road used to very popular with local youths, who used it as a drag strip. As a number of car crash deaths occurred on this stretch of road, stories started to be bandied about a "ghost car". Could the reports of the aforementioned "ghostly headlights" have any connection with this "ghost car"?

22. Fisher's Ghost

One of the most popular ghost stories ever to come out of Australia involves a certain farmer by the name of Frederick Fisher.

One quiet June evening in 1826, Fisher left his house in Campbelltown to run some errands. Mysteriously, he never ever returned. He seemed to have just vanished without a trace, and there were no clues that could account for his sudden disappearance.

Four months after Fisher vanished, a local resident stumbled into a Campbelltown hotel, pale-faced and shaking with shock. He told the people in the hotel that he had just encountered the ghost of Frederick Fisher. The phantom farmer had been sitting on a fence by the road, pointing with his finger at a paddock near the river that ran nearby. Then man watched in disbelief as the apparition faded away into thin air before his stunned gaze.

The man who had witnessed the ghost was quite an affluent and well-respected member of the local community, so the police decided to investigate the paddock at which the ghost had pointed. Much to their shock, they discovered the dead body of Frederick Fisher. His murderer was a man called George Worrall, Fisher's neighbour and friend who had been taking care of his legal matters in the past. Worrall had already set some people's tongues wagging after Fisher's disappearance, as he told everybody that Fisher had sailed to England and soon started selling off the poor farmer's belongings. The discovery of the body soon led to Worrall making a full confession, and Fisher could finally rest in peace.

But has Fisher's spirit really gone for good? Some sources say that Fisher quite enjoyed being a ghost . . . to the extent that his spirit still haunts the hotel mentioned in the legend to this very day.

23. Tomago House

Tomago House is a well-known building of a large vineyard in Newcastle, New South Wales. Construction work began on the site in 1840. However, its builder, barrister Richard Windeyer, died just seven years later. He was survived by his wife, Maria, who now took charge of completing the site and making it profitable.

Maria really devoted herself to this task, and spent the rest of her life looking after Tomago House. She added a chapel to the property between 1860 and 1861.

Maria's life and spirit became so closely linked with Tomago House that some say her interest in the property didn't really end with her death. To this day, many people have reported seeing the elderly woman walking around in the cellars, or enjoying fresh air in her rocking chair on the porch of the house.

Maria's ghost has actually become something of a tourist attraction, and ghost tours are regularly held at Tomago House by such organisations as the Newcastle Ghost Tours.

Maria Windeyer died in the 19th Century.

24. Dreamworld Theme Park

When Australia screened its first season of Big Brother in 2001 from a studio at Dreamworld Theme Park, there were a number of paranormal incidents witnessed by a number of people there.

The building is reported to be haunted by the ghost of a little girl. She is said to appear at sunrise and sunset, and has apparently been seen by both crew and cast members of the show.

Also, there is a male ghost who likes to frighten visitors on the Buzzsaw ride, which opened in 2011. The ride is based around apparitions of the phantom of a man called Jack Darke, who was killed by a buzz saw during the time of the gold rush. His death, however, was covered up by the town. There have been several reports that the real ghost of Jack Drake has attached himself to the theme park and often appears to patrons during the ride.

25. The Min Min Lights

The phenomenon known as "ghost lights" has been reported from all corners of the globe for many years. These strange luminosities have also been called will-o'-the-wisps, Jack o'lanterns and fairy lights. Australia has had more than its fair share of such stories, and the most famous is that of the "Min Min Lights". The majority of the sightings have occurred in Channel Country.

The Min Min Lights are named after a very small settlement which comprised of an email exchange, a pub and a small cemetery which once stood on the boundary of two big stations: Warenda and Lucknow, near the town of Boulia, South West Queensland. In the 1800's the pub burnt down, and very little of the original small settlement still stands.

The first official reported sighting of the Min Min Lights occurred in the Sunday Mail magazine, March 2nd, 1941, although there have since been other reports even earlier than that. Around 10.00 pm, as the stockman passed by the Min Min area, a weird glow appeared in the centre of the little cemetery located at the rear of the hotel. The glow grew to the size of a small watermelon, hovered for a few moments over the graveyard, then moved off in the same direction that the stockman was going. Startled by this strange luminosity, the stockman galloped towards Boulia, with the light chasing him all the way, until he finally reached town.

The weird glow usually starts off as one light, sometimes two, sometimes several, and sometimes as hundreds of tiny lights. It may linger for a few minutes, or even hours. Sometimes it is static, sometimes it travels as fast as a speeding vehicle. It usually hovers about a metre from the ground, and has been known to jump or float along fences. It often appears high in the sky, occasionally bobbing up and down like some weird yo-yo. It differs from a headlight in that it casts its light around all its sides. Although it usually appears as a strange but harmless light, it has occasionally frightened people who have encountered it.

The most frequent sightings of the Min Min Lights occurred between 1950 and 1959, with only 12 between 1940 - 49 and 16 in the following decade.

There have been many hypotheses put forward for the Min Min Lights phenomenon. For instance, some people reckon they could be luminescent insects (genus and species unknown) in a ball of breeding frenzy. Others believe they are spirits of the deceased, returning to earth to warn and give guidance. Another possible explanation for these lights is that they could be fireballs, electrical disturbances, or meteorites.

The Min Min lights have even been connected with UFOs, but both the appearance and behaviour of this phenomenon bears little similarity to the typical UFO sighting.

A rather sinister and ominous story surrounds the Min Min Lights: it is said that anybody who chases and catches them will never return to tell the tale.

26. Fortuna Villa

Fortuna Villa is a mansion near Bendigo in Victoria, Australia. It was built in 1855, during the gold rush. In WWII, the Australian Army used the house as a mapping survey centre. Later on, it was declared the property of the Victorian Parliament and became a listed Commonwealth Heritage site.

Fortuna Villa is said to be home to many ghosts: the bearded spirit of George Lansell, one of the owners and a founder of Bendigo; the ghost of a teenage girl reportedly appears, asking people to leave; strange footsteps can be heard late at night, as well as the tapping of a cane, and in some rooms cold spots are felt.

In 1986, a person saw a dark shape, without legs, passing right through the banister of the main staircase. Also, some claim to have heard a female voice, supposedly that of Bedilia, Lansell's first wife, who died in mysterious circumstances. Some military personnel, stationed in the mapping survey centre, have reported that previously locked doors are found open, and a boy dressed in a sailor suit appeared to a female soldier, vanishing when she called out for help.

Members of the Australian Army wrote a letter to their superiors asking for relocation out of the property due to these persistent hauntings. As expected, their request was denied.

27. Macquarie Fields Railway Station

Macquarie Fields Railway Station is situated in the south-western suburbs of Sydney and is situated on the Main South Line. It is served by Sydney Trains of the Airport, Inner West and South and Cumberland lines. It serves a residential area, and opened in 1888.

It is said that late at night, when the station is nearly empty, you can often hear the ghostly moans and groans of a young girl in her teens. The paranormal occurrence starts with spine-chilling screams, which become much louder. Someone once reported that they saw a young girl wearing dancing clothes, covered in what appeared to be blood in her chest area. She was also described as actually clutching her chest.

The ghost girl lurks around the station moaning and groaning. She has also been seen sitting in the middle of the station, where she just stares vacuously into space and sobs.

For all the creepiness of her appearance and sounds, the phantom girl does appear to be relatively harmless, as nobody has reported any menacing behaviour from this apparition.

28. Manly Quarantine Station

The Manly Quarantine Station dates back to 1828, a period when disease-ridden ships docked in Australia from all corners of the globe. The Quarantine Station was specially set up to prevent the spread of deadly illnesses like Spanish Influenza and smallpox. Thousands of new arrivals were forced to stay there for months, often living in very squalid conditions.

The spirits of the numerous people who died from disease and neglect are said to haunt the now disused Quarantine buildings. Visitors to the site have witnessed many incidents of paranormal activity, including cold spots, mysterious lights, ominous feelings, and the spirits of the deceased workers and patients.

Among these apparitions is the presence of a girl with blonde plaited hair, who has been witnessed speaking to visitors, often even taking them by the hand.

Another strange phenomenon is when visitors to the building have suddenly felt their nostrils being assailed by strong, unexplained smells, the odour of lemon and potato being especially common.

29. The Supermarket Ghost

At an IGA store in Brompton, South Australia, a new security camera has captured strange goings on, which suggest that a ghost may be haunting the premises - a ghost that seems to have a predilection for Fruit Roll Ups.

The security camera filmed a packet of Fruit Roll Ups being tossed between 18 and 36 feet away from its original location, despite the fact that nobody was around at the time. The camera has also shown how one box mysteriously jumped six meters from its original location on the floor of the IGA store in Adelaide, despite no one being present.

When owner Norm Hurst bought the store in October, he was told to expect the occurrence of some supernatural activity. He had been told by the previous owner that the store was haunted. At first he was cynical, but once strange things did indeed start to happen in his store - especially the incident with the Fruit Roll Ups - he soon changed his mind.

What shocked Hurst the most was the sheer force with which the Roll Ups were thrown. One of the cameras shows the packet of Roll-Ups just arriving on the ground: it had not just slid off; it had been thrown out of the pasta, yet the Roll-Ups were kept 12 metres away.

The actual cause of the mysterious activity at the IGA is still unknown, but one theory suggested by the stars of the Australian morning talk show, Sunrise On 7, is that it's connected with the 1998 death of a boxer who was shot on the sidewalk just outside the store.

30. Phantom Kangaroos

We all know that kangaroos, along with koala bears and wallabies, are native to Australia. However, strange occurrences of kangaroos appearing in areas where they are not normally found are sometimes reported. They have even been sighted in places as far away as North America. Often they appear ghost-like, vanishing into thin air or hopping right through walls.

Some of these weird kangaroo sightings sound exactly like normal kangaroos. Other sightings describe giant kangaroos, ghostly kangaroos, kangaroos that oddly resemble dogs, or kangaroos with uncharacteristically monstrous habits, like slaughtering and feeding on sheep.

The weirder kangaroo reports are sometimes classed as actually being reports of giant monkeys, because the upper bodies of these creatures are described as resembling those of simians. Other reports are classified as chupacabras, a legendary cryptid rumoured to inhabit parts of the Americas, with the first sightings reported in Puerto Rico. The name comes from the animal's tendency to attack and drink the blood of livestock.

The term "phantom kangaroo" is frequently used for all types of cryptid kangaroos, regardless of how normal or strange the creature in question is. The term "phantom kangaroo" is quite similar to "phantom cat," which is widely used for reports of eastern cougars and mystery black panthers, regardless of whether the cats in question are attributed with ghostly characteristics or seem solidly physical.

Some paranormal experts believe that these strange kangaroo-like entities are aliens or spirits haunting us from another dimension. Someone suggested animal teleportation. Maybe they even bounce in and out of this physical world.

Whatever their origin, these phantom kangaroos are said to be an omen – an ominous warning that you will soon be encountering the supernatural.

If you enjoyed this book and would like to sign up for Alan Toner's Newsletter to keep up date with his new book releases and current writing projects, you can do so by going to his official website at www.wirralwriter.co.uk and clicking on the Subscribe link.

You might also like to check out his other website, True Ghost Stories, at: www.trueghoststories.co.uk

Printed in Great Britain
by Amazon